133
CON

Date Due

MAR 28	TAM LUU	6-204
APR 4	Alice Chan	6-205
APR 18	DAVID E	6206
	J. Underwood	
NOV 14	Lily Tang	124
FEB 6	Jenny No	103
MAR 20	Allegra Wilson	6-206
OCT 21	Jose Lemus	6-25
NOV 27	Sabola Mackey	30-1
JAN 5	Bonnie Wong	304

GHOSTS AND THE SUPERNATURAL

EDWINA CONNER

The Bookwright Press
New York · 1987

Topics

Cover *The three witches in Macbeth* by Charles Folleard (1911).

All the words that appear
in **bold** are explained in the
glossary on page 30.

First published in the
United States in 1987 by
The Bookwright Press
387 Park Avenue South
New York, NY 10016

First published in 1987 by
Wayland (Publishers) Limited
61 Western Road, Hove
East Sussex, BN3 1JD, England

© Copyright 1987 Wayland (Publishers) Ltd

ISBN 0–531–18150–2
Library of Congress Catalog Card Number: 86–73065

Phototypeset by
Kalligraphics Ltd, Redhill, Surrey
Printed in Belgium by
Casterman sa, Tournai

10.90

Contents

Doomed to Walk the Earth

Borley Rectory, a famous haunted house in England where people claimed to see ghosts and evidence of poltergeists. The house has since burned down.

Do you believe in ghosts? Would you spend a night alone in a haunted house? You might risk running into, or rather through, one somewhere along a creaking corridor. It is not only castles that are said to have ghosts. The Society for **Psychical** Research keeps records of all kinds of reported hauntings in houses, schools, offices

This ghostly headless dog appeared on the photograph of ladies having tea.

and churches, as well as on lonely country paths and in busy city streets.

In many societies and from very early times, men and women have feared the return of their dead ancestors, or others, who they thought were not allowed to rest in peace and so were forced to pace the earth, seeking revenge on whoever had done them wrong.

Ghosts were once thought of as devils or monsters and were

One of the most famous ghosts in literature: Hamlet sees the ghost of his recently murdered father.

described by their terrified victims as "horned giants," or as strange, cruel animals breathing fire. Today, however, people who study ghosts think that many look like you and me: solid and human.

Sometimes the ghost of a dying or recently dead person "appears" to friends and relatives. Other ghosts haunt one place and appear to strangers and friends alike. One country clergyman reported that a tall man, dressed as a priest, came regularly to worship at his church. He thought little of this until one day he "bumped" into the man and walked straight through him.

In Dickens' book A Christmas Carol, *the ghost of Marley appears to Scrooge and begs him to give up his miserly ways.*

A pan, lid and scissors appear to fly through the air. Are poltergeists responsible for such happenings?

Some ghosts are particularly frightening. One manor in England is said to be haunted by a woman with great hollows instead of eyes, and in one English churchyard you might come across a woman with no face. Ghosts of people who have suffered a violent death are believed to show signs of how they died. Under a bridge in New Orleans, there is said to stalk the spirit of a man who drowned, dripping with ghostly seaweed.

The mischievous ghosts responsible for hurling objects around the room are known as **poltergeists**. In the past such happenings were put down to witchcraft. Nowadays some experts think that the acts of poltergeists are due to **psychokinesis**, the power of the human mind to make objects move.

Many people claim to have seen a ghost, but *proving* that you've seen one is not at all easy!

"Double, Double, Toil and Trouble"

The witches in Macbeth stir their magic brew and chant a spell.

This is a line in a magic spell spoken by the three **witches** in William Shakespeare's play, *Macbeth*. This play was written in about 1605, when witchcraft and witch hunting were common throughout Europe.

Witches have always been either "white" or "black." "White" witches helped people with their **supernatural** powers, but "black" witches were thought to use the power of the Devil.

They put curses on people, sank ships, destroyed crops and generally caused chaos.

A group of witches is called a **coven**. Twelve witches plus the Devil form a coven, which is why the number 13 is thought to be unlucky. Witches held meetings, called **witches' sabbats**. To get there, they were said to fly on broomsticks, perhaps accompanied by their "familiars," or magic

Three witches with their "familiars," or magic animals.

Anne Baker

Ioane Willimott

Ellen Greene

animals, usually cats. Some people believed that witches ate the flesh of children and mixed potions to charm and curse their victims.

"The Witches' Home," a dramatic imaginary scene painted in the nineteenth century.

From the fifteenth to the seventeenth century, witch hunting was widespread in Europe. In 1644, a lawyer called Matthew Hopkins set himself up as "Witch Finder General." He traveled around, England, seeking out witches and torturing them horribly. When they "confessed" he executed them.

One of Hopkins' tests for discovering witches (usually women) was to bind the poor victim's left hand to her right foot and her right hand to her left foot and duck her in a lake or pond. If she sank she was innocent, and if she floated she was a witch and was executed. Sometimes an "innocent" woman was hauled up before she drowned, but often it was too late.

A woman in England in the early seventeenth century, being lowered into the water to "prove" whether or not she is a witch.

Some witches were "exorcised" instead of executed. This meant that a priest would perform a religious ceremony to drive the Devil out of her body.

Two things are clear about witchcraft at this time: first, there were people who claimed to be witches and practice magic, and second, there were people who did not claim to be witches but were still

An artist's impression of the Salem Witch Trials in Massachusetts in 1692.

This Voodoo dancer is drawing magical signs on the ground.

accused, tried, condemned and executed.

Witch hunting spread to America. In 1692, nineteen men and women were hanged as witches in Salem, Massachusetts.

Voodoo is a form of African witchcraft that traveled to the West Indies with the black slaves. The island of Haiti is still the most important center of Voodoo. Voodoo ceremonies are performed by priests and priestesses who claim to be possessed by spirits. These spirits send the priests and priestesses into trances and make them perform wild dances. Voodoo witch doctors can put curses on people, but they may also try to heal the sick with herbal medicines and magic. Sticking pins into a model of the cursed person is still a common way for a witch doctor to inflict torture. **Zombies** – dead people recalled to life but without a soul – are part of Voodoo belief.

Vampires and Werewolves

Imagine traveling in a horse-drawn coach through the gloomy landscape of Transylvania, a country in eastern Europe. There is a fearful storm, the wind howls, the rain pours down, lightning flashes across the sky. High above looms the evil-looking castle you are

Count Dracula, as seen in one of the many film versions of the famous vampire story.

going to visit. The coach driver, terrified, refuses to take you to the door, so you trudge through the mud and finally arrive, soaking wet, at the vast wooden door of the castle. You ring the ancient bell. After a minute or two the door opens a crack, then swings back, creaking loudly . . . you step inside and find yourself face to face with – Count Dracula!

When Bram Stoker wrote the story of Dracula, in the late ninteenth century, it was immediately popular and has since provided the theme for many horror films.

Count Dracula is the world's most famous **vampire**. Vampires are the "undead" beings who feed on the blood of living people. They are supposed to be corpses who rise from their graves at nightfall and spend the hours of darkness seeking out sleeping men and women so they can sink their fangs into their

This castle in Romania is traditionally believed to have belonged to Count Dracula.

victims' necks and suck their blood.

Vampires must be back in the grave before dawn or else they dissolve and melt into a puddle. The only other ways to get rid of a vampire are to burn it or to find its coffin during the daylight hours and drive a wooden stake through its heart.

All vampires were said to hate the sight of an image of Christ on the Cross, so this symbol was a powerful weapon against them. Wearing garlic was also thought to keep vampires away.

One of the popular beliefs about vampires is that they hate and fear the sight of Christ on the Cross.

"The Vampire of Groglin Grange" – another creature from a horror story.

Werewolves also like feeding on human blood – and flesh. Werewolves are ordinary human beings who (particularly on nights when there is a full moon) have the unfortunate habit of turning into enormous wolves, running amok and setting upon anyone unlucky enough to be in their path.

There are, of course, *real* wolves and *real* vampire bats, but belief in *human* vampires and werewolves is merely superstition and has no basis in fact.

But, in the past, frightened and ignorant people sometimes thought they had evidence of the existence of vampires and werewolves. In the sixteenth century, for example, a Frenchman called Giles Garnier was thought to be a werewolf. Under torture he "confessed," admitting that he ate children when he was in the shape of a wolf. Many others accused of witchcraft died as he did – burned at the stake.

A supposed werewolf in seventeenth-century Germany. In the center you can see him falling into a well and on the left he is being hanged.

The Fairy Ring

It may sound strange, but many people believe in **fairies**. There are all kinds of Wee Folk: elves, goblins, hobgoblins, dwarfs, pixies and many others. Some fairies are tiny, some human sized, others about the height of young children.

Traditionally, fairies have many practical skills: they keep fairy cattle, pigs and dogs and are

Fairy "photos" like this astonished people when they first appeared, but they are known to be clever fakes.

especially good at weaving and spinning. They often "borrow" clothes and food from humans and reward people who are kind to them by leaving delicious fairy cakes for them to eat.

Many fairies have magical powers – remember the Wicked Fairy and the Fairy Godmother in the story of Sleeping Beauty? The Wicked Fairy was not invited to the princess's christening, so she put a curse on the tiny baby: she would

Sleeping Beauty, about to be awakened by the prince.

grow up to be a beautiful girl but would then prick her finger and die. Then the Fairy Godmother came along and did her best to help. She changed the spell so the princess would not die, but would sleep for a hundred years until kissed by the handsome prince.

Goblins tend to be mischievous and evil, though hobgoblins are

A crowd of rather fierce goblins and many other strange small folk.

supposed to be kinder to humans.
All fairies have a strong sense of
right and wrong. A Pwca (Pooka) is
a mischievous Welsh fairy,
sometimes shown as a little tadpole-
like creature. One story tells how a
milkmaid used to leave a bowl of
milk and a piece of bread out for
Pwca every day. Once she drank

*"The Elf King
Asleep": the idea of
people as small as
insects has often
fascinated writers and
painters.*

Peter Pan – one of the most popular of the fairy characters in children's stories.

the milk herself and left only the crust of the bread. Next day she felt something grip her hands tightly and she received an invisible, but painful, whipping from the furious fairy.

Pwca is also known as Will o' the Wisp. He is supposed to lead a person who is lost up a narrow path to the edge of a cliff, then leap over it, laughing loudly, blowing out his candle and leaving the poor wanderer to try to find a way home.

Mysteries of the Mind

Have you ever dreamed about an event and then found out that it really has happened? Or perhaps you've guessed what someone was about to say before they said it? If so, you may be using **extrasensory perception (ESP)**. This is the ability

Tarot cards, like these in this old French pack, are used to foretell the future.

This fortuneteller claims to see future events reflected in the crystal ball.

to know something without using any of our five senses (of sight, hearing, touch, taste and smell).

People who claim to see into the future – prophets, soothsayers and fortunetellers – have existed in all countries for thousands of years. Today fortunetellers use many ways of looking into the future, such as tarot cards, crystal balls or palmistry (looking at a person's hand and "reading" the lines on it).

Some people claim they are **clairvoyant**, that is they can "know" things using a special "sixth" sense. In one story, for example, a woman suddenly jumped up at a dinner party and insisted on being driven home. When she got to her house she found it was on fire with her invalid husband trapped in the flames. He was rescued just in time. This woman was not aware that she was clairvoyant; she just sensed that something was terribly wrong.

This Japanese man uses bundles of sticks to tell people's fortunes.

President Abraham Lincoln was supposed to have dreamed that he was lying in his coffin a few days before he was assassinated in 1865.

Some people seem to be **telepathic** – they can tell what another person is thinking. Scientists have tested this by putting two people in separate rooms and getting one to pick, from a selection, the shape that the other person has just selected. Even allowing for the possibility of chance, it seems clear that many people do have a gift for sensing what another person is thinking.

Faith healers, such as this woman, claim to have special powers to make sick people well.

A man called Uri Geller made headlines a few years ago by apparently being able to bend metal objects, such as spoons, without touching them. He seemed only to use the power of his mind. This power is called psychokinesis.

Another version of ESP is the so-called ability to receive messages from the dead. A **medium** (a person who claims to have this gift) may charge a fee to hold a **séance** and deliver messages from the spirits of the dead to their relatives, even though the medium has never met the dead person or any of the people who come to the séance.

It's hard to say whether any of these examples of **parapsychology** are genuine or simply tricks, coincidences or delusions, but so many reports of such incidents come from perfectly sane and normal people that it is impossible to dismiss them all as nonsense.

Doris Stokes, a modern English medium, "talks" to people who have died and passes messages to their families.

Glossary

Clairvoyant Able to "know" about objects and events without using the usual senses of sight, hearing, touch, smell or taste. A person with this ability.

Coven An assembly of witches.

Extrasensory perception (ESP) Any method of "knowing" that involves a special "sixth" sense. Clairvoyance and telepathy are kinds of ESP.

Fairies Tiny creatures who live in a world we cannot see. They may be friendly or mischievous.

Ghost The spirit of a dead person.

Medium Someone through whom the spirits of the dead supposedly communicate.

Parapsychology The study of such things as telepathy and clairvoyance.

Poltergeist A mischievous spirit that likes to hurl furniture and ornaments around the room.

Psychical To do with the world of ghosts, spirits and ESP.

Psychokinesis Moving objects without touching them, using only the power of the mind.

Séance A meeting at which people try to get messages from the dead.

Supernatural Belonging to a world above and beyond our everyday physical one.

Telepathic Able to read another person's mind.

Vampire An "undead" monster that sucks the blood of living human beings.

Voodoo A form of African witchcraft.

Werewolf A person who turns into a wolf at certain times.

Witch A person who uses, or is believed to use, magic powers to perform either good or evil. Evil witches are said to have sold their souls to the Devil.

Witches' sabbat A gathering of witches and demons.

Zombie A corpse that is brought back to life, but has no soul. Part of Voodoo belief.

Books to Read

America's Very Own Ghosts, by Daniel Cohen. Dodd, 1985.

A Book of Ghosts, by Pam Adams and Ceri Jones. Playspaces, 1974.

Devils and Demons, by Rhonda Blumberg. Franklin Watts, 1982.

Ghosts, Witches and Things like That, by Roderick Hunt. Merrimack Publishing Circle, 1985.

Haunted House, by Larry Kettelkamp. Morrow, William and Co., 1969.

Learning More About Ghosts, by Slylvia Tester. Children's Press, 1981.

Super Stitches: A Book of Superstitions, by Ann Nevins. Holiday House, Inc., 1983.

Witches and Witchcraft, by Adrienne Jack. Franklin Watts, 1981.

Witchcraft of Salem Village, by Shirley Jackson. Random House, 1956.

Picture Acknowledgments
The illustrations in this book were supplied by: Barnaby's Picture Library 14, 16, 26; BPCC/Aldus Archive 8, 13, 18, 23, 25, 27; Bridgeman Art Library 7, 11 (Victoria and Albert Museum); E.T. Archive 21; Fortean Picture Library 5; Mansell Collection 12, 19; Mary Evans Picture Library 4, 6, 17, 20, 22, 24, 28; National Film Archive 15; Topham Picture Library 29. Artwork on page 9 is by Richard Hook. All other pictures are from the Wayland Picture Library.

Index